iPhone®

FOR

DUMMIES®

A Wiley Brand

Mini Edition

by Edward C. Baig

USA TODAY Personal Tech columnist

and

Bob LeVitus

Houston Chronicle "Dr. Mac" columnist

FOR

DUMMIES®

A Wiley Brand

iPhone® For Dummies®, Mini Edition

Published by
John Wiley & Sons, Inc.
111 River Street
Hoboken, NJ 07030-5774
www.wiley.com

Copyright © 2014 by John Wiley & Sons, Inc., Hoboken, New Jersey

Published by John Wiley & Sons, Inc., Hoboken, New Jersey

Published simultaneously in Canada

For general information on our other products and services, please contact our Customer Care Department within the U.S. at 877-762-2974, outside the U.S. at 317-572-3993, or fax 317-572-4002.

For technical support, please visit www.wiley.com/techsupport.

Wiley publishes in a variety of print and electronic formats and by print-on-demand. Some material included with standard print versions of this book may not be included in e-books or in print-on-demand. If this book refers to media such as a CD or DVD that is not included in the version you purchased, you may download this material at http://booksupport.wiley.com. For more information about Wiley products, visit www.wiley.com.

ISBN: 978-1-118-74452-9

Manufactured in the United States of America

10 9 8 7 6 5 4 3 2 1

Publisher's Acknowledgments

Project Editor:
Charlotte Kughen

Executive Editor: Bob Woerner

Editorial Manager: Jodi Jensen

Editorial Assistant:
Anne Sullivan

Senior Project Coordinator:
Kristie Rees

Contents

Introduction

● ●

*P*recious few products ever come close to generating the kind of buzz seen with the iPhone 5s. Its messianic arrival received front-page treatment in newspapers and top billing on network and cable TV shows. People lined up days in advance just to ensure landing one of the first units. Years from now, people will insist, "I was one of them."

But we trust you didn't pick up this book to read yet another account about how the iPhone 5s launch was an epochal event. We trust you *did* buy the book to find out how to get the most out of your remarkable device. Our goal is to deliver that information in a light and breezy fashion. We expect you to have fun using your iPhone 5s. We equally hope you have fun spending time with us.

About This Book

As with most Apple products, the iPhone is beautifully designed and intuitive to use. And although our editors may not want us to reveal this dirty little secret (especially on the first page, for goodness' sake), the truth is that you'll get pretty far just by exploring the iPhone's many functions and features on your own. But this little book is chock-full of useful tips, advice, and other nuggets that should make your iPhone experience even more pleasurable.

At the time we wrote this book, the information contained within was accurate for the iPhone 5s and the latest versions of iTunes and the iPhone OS (operating system), known as iOS 7.

If you want to explore other aspects of the iPhone that we couldn't cover here, please check out *iPhone For Dummies*, 7th Edition, from John Wiley & Sons.

Icons Used in This Book

The following icons appear in the left margins throughout this book; they tell you something extra about the topic at hand or hammer a point home:

 These are the juicy morsels, shortcuts, and recommendations that might make the task at hand faster or easier.

 This icon emphasizes the stuff we think you ought to retain. You may even jot down a note to yourself in the iPhone.

 Ignoring warnings may be hazardous to your iPhone and (by extension) your wallet.

Part I

iPhone Basic Training

●●●●●●●●●●●●●●●●●●●●●●●●●●●●●●●

In This Part

▶ Taking a tour of the iPhone

▶ Getting used to the multitouch interface

▶ Trying out Cut, Copy, Paste, and Replace

▶ Using the Control Center

▶ Organizing your stuff with folders

▶ Shooting photos and video

●●●●●●●●●●●●●●●●●●●●●●●●●●●●●●●

*I*n addition to being a killer cellphone, the iPhone 5s (and its less-expensive brother, the iPhone 5c) is a gorgeous widescreen video iPod, a convenient 8-megapixel camera/camcorder, and a small, powerful Internet communications device (and we haven't even mentioned everything it can do with apps that you add).

In this tiny book, we don't have room to cover every aspect of this fabulous device. But the following sections help you get familiar with your iPhone and some of what it can do.

Technical Specifications

Here's a list of everything you need before you can actually *use* your iPhone with iOS 7:

- ✔ An iPhone (4, 4s, 5, or 5s/5c)

- ✔ In the United States, a wireless contract with AT&T, Sprint, or Verizon (available carriers vary with iPhone model)

- ✔ An Apple ID (which you can set up for free)

- ✔ Internet access (required) — broadband wireless Internet access recommended

Plus you need *one* of the following:

- ✔ A Mac with a USB 2.0 port; OS X version 10.8 or later (some features require OS X Mavericks); and iTunes 11.0 or later

- ✔ A PC with a USB 2.0 port; Windows 7 or Windows 8r; and iTunes 11.0 or later

A Quick Tour Outside

The iPhone is a harmonious combination of hardware and software — read on.

On the top

Here's what you'll find on the top of your iPhone (see Figure 1-1):

- ✔ **Sleep/Wake button:** Use this button to lock or unlock your iPhone and to turn your iPhone on or off. When locked, you can still receive calls and text messages, but nothing happens if you touch the screen. When turned off, all incoming calls go to voicemail.

Sleep/Wake button

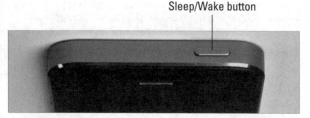

Figure 1-1: Top of iPhone 5s.

On the bottom

Here's what you'll find on the bottom of your iPhone (see Figure 1-2):

- ✔ **Speaker:** Used by the iPhone's built-in speakerphone and plays audio if no headset is plugged in. It also plays the ringtone you hear when you receive a call.

Microphone   Speaker
Headset jack Lightning connector

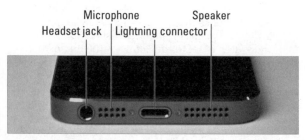

Figure 1-2: Bottom of iPhone 5s.

- **Headset jack:** The headset jack lets you plug in the included iPhone headset that has a microphone and remote so that you can talk as well as listen.

- **Lightning connector:** The Lightning connector has two purposes. One, you can use it to recharge your iPhone's battery by connecting one end of the included cable to the Lightning connector and the other end to AC power via the USB power adapter. Two, you can use the Lightning connector to synchronize data between your iPhone and your computer (which also charges your iPhone, but more slowly). Connect one end of the same cable to the Lightning connector and the other end to a USB port on your Mac or PC.

- **Microphone:** The microphone lets callers hear your voice when you're not using a headset.

On the sides and front

On the front of your iPhone, you'll find the following (see Figure 1-3):

- **Ring/Silent switch:** This switch lets you quickly switch between ring mode and silent mode. When the switch is set to ring mode — the up position — your iPhone plays all sounds through the speaker on the bottom. When the switch is set to silent mode — the down position — your iPhone doesn't make a sound when you receive a call or when a notification pops up on the screen. (It can, however, be set to vibrate to alert you of an incoming call or notification.)

If you want to silence your phone quickly, press the sleep/wake button on the top of the iPhone or press one of the volume buttons.

- ✔ **Volume buttons:** Two volume buttons are just below the ring/silent switch on the left side. The upper button increases the volume; the lower one decreases it.

- ✔ **SIM card tray:** On the iPhone 4/4s/5/5s/5c, the SIM card tray is on the right side; this is where you remove or replace the SIM card inside your iPhone.

- ✔ **Camera:** The camera on the front of the iPhone 4, 4s, 5, 5s/5c is tuned for FaceTime, so it has just the right field of view and focal length to focus on your face at arm's length.

- ✔ **Microphone:** Used for FaceTime calls and noise suppression during phone calls. (See Part II for more about FaceTime.)

- ✔ **Receiver:** This is the speaker the iPhone uses for telephone calls.

- ✔ **Status bar:** The status bar displays important information such as signal and battery strength.

- ✔ **Touchscreen:** You find out how to use the iPhone's gorgeous high-resolution color touch-screen later in this part.

- ✔ **Home button:** Press the Home button at any time to display the Home screen. Talk about high-tech — the Home button on the iPhone 5s includes a new fingerprint sensor that can unlock your iPhone when you pass your thumb over it.

- ✔ **App buttons:** Each button on the Home screen launches an included iPhone app or one you've acquired from the App Store.

Volume buttons
Ring/Silent switch
App buttons Status bar
Receiver

Home button
Touchscreen

Figure 1-3: The front of the iPhone 5s.

On the back

On the back of your iPhone is the camera lens. It's the little circle in the top-left corner. Next to the camera lens is a little LED that's used as a flash for photos and a floodlight for videos (as well as a flashlight). There's also yet another microphone for capturing sound while you're shooting video.

Home Sweet Home Screen

To get to your Home screen, press the Home button. If your iPhone is asleep when you press, the unlock screen appears, where you enter your passcode (or use your thumbprint) to unlock the device. After it's unlocked, the phone shows whichever page of icons was on the screen when it went to sleep.

Three steps let you rearrange icons on your iPhone:

1. **Press and hold any icon until all the icons begin to jiggle.**

2. **Drag the icons around until you're happy with their positions.**

3. **Press the Home button to save your arrangement and stop the jiggling.**

If you haven't rearranged your icons, you see the following applications on your Home screen, starting at the top left (depending on the iOS version you're using, your iPhone may have a different number of icons):

- **Messages:** Lets you exchange text and multimedia messages with almost any other cellphone user. You can also take advantage of *iMessages*, which enable you to send free text, photo, and video messages with Mac computers running OS X Lion, Mountain Lion, and Mavericks (as well as other iOS 5, 6, and 7 devices).

- **Calendar:** Lets you synchronize events and alerts between your computer and iPhone if you use OS X Calendar or Microsoft Entourage, Outlook, or Exchange as the calendar program on your PC or Mac.

- ✔ **Photos:** Lets you view pictures that you took with the iPhone's built-in camera or transferred from your computer.

- ✔ **Camera:** Lets you shoot a picture or video with the 5-megapixel (iPhone 4) or 8-megapixel (iPhone 4s, 5, and 5s/5c) built-in camera.

- ✔ **Weather:** Monitors the six-day weather forecast for as many cities as you choose.

- ✔ **Clock:** Lets you see the current time in as many cities as you like, set one or more alarms, and use your iPhone as a stopwatch or a countdown timer.

- ✔ **Maps:** Enables you to view street maps or satellite imagery of locations around the globe, ask for directions, check traffic conditions, or find a nearby pizza joint.

- ✔ **Videos:** Launches an app so you can watch movies, TV shows, and music videos.

- ✔ **Notes:** Lets you type notes that you can save to your iPhone or e-mail to yourself or anyone else.

- ✔ **Reminders:** Saves your to-do list, complete with visual and audio reminders.

- ✔ **Stocks:** Monitors the performance of your favorite stocks, and helps you catch up on the latest financial news.

- ✔ **Game Center:** Ready to play a game? The Game Center makes it easy to locate friends for a quick challenge, or review your achievements.

- ✔ **Newsstand:** If you're familiar with iBooks — Apple's ebook reader — then you'll feel right at home with this periodical and newspaper reader. (It even updates your subscriptions automatically.)

- ✔ **iTunes Store:** Gives you access to the iTunes Store.
- ✔ **App Store:** Enables you to connect to and search the iTunes App Store.
- ✔ **Passbook:** Stores your airplane boarding passes, event tickets, and store coupons and loyalty cards for easy retrieval.
- ✔ **Compass:** Uses your iPhone's built-in GPS and Wi-Fi to provide an accurate real-time compass.
- ✔ **Settings:** Lets you adjust various settings on your iPhone.
- ✔ **Phone:** Enables you to use the iPhone as a phone. What a concept!
- ✔ **Mail:** Lets you send and receive e-mail with most e-mail systems.
- ✔ **Safari:** Lets you surf the web with this browser.
- ✔ **Music:** Unleashes all the power of a video iPod right on your phone.

Now that you and your iPhone have been properly introduced, it's time to turn it on, activate it, and actually use it. Onward!

Mastering the Multitouch Interface

With the iPhone, the usual physical buttons on your phone are replaced by a *multitouch display*. The iPhone includes six keyboard layouts in English, all variations on the alphabetical keyboard, the numeric and punctuation keyboard, and the more punctuation and symbols keyboard. The layout you see depends on the application you are working in.

The iPhone keyboard contains six keys that don't actually type a character:

- ✔ **Shift key:** On the alphabetical keyboard, the Shift key switches between uppercase and lowercase letters. On the other two keyboards, pressing Shift switches you to the one you're not currently using.

 To turn on Caps Lock mode and type all caps, you first need to enable Caps Lock. Tap the Settings icon, tap General, and then tap Keyboard. Tap the Enable Caps Lock item to turn it on. After the Caps Lock setting is enabled (it's disabled by default), you double-tap the Shift key to turn on Caps Lock. (The Shift key turns blue when Caps Lock is on.) Tap the Shift key again to turn off Caps Lock. To disable Caps Lock completely, just reverse the process by turning off the Enable Caps Lock setting (tap Settings, General, Keyboard).

- ✔ **Toggle key:** Switches between the different keyboard layouts.
- ✔ **Dictation key:** Types the words you speak.
- ✔ **International keyboard key:** Shows up only if you've turned on an international keyboard.
- ✔ **Delete key:** Erases the character immediately to the left of the cursor.
- ✔ **Return key:** Moves the cursor to the beginning of the next line.

The virtual iPhone keyboard

Here's why this keyboard is so smart:

- ✔ Includes a built-in English dictionary with words from today's popular culture.

- ✔ Adds your contacts to its dictionary automatically.

- ✔ Uses complex analysis algorithms to predict the word you're trying to type.

- ✔ Suggests corrections as you type. It then offers you the suggested word just below the word you typed. When you decline a suggestion and the word you typed is *not* in the iPhone dictionary, the iPhone adds that word to its dictionary and offers it as a suggestion in the future.

 Be sure to decline suggestions by tapping the characters you typed as opposed to the suggested words that appear beneath what you've typed; doing so helps your intelligent keyboard become even smarter.

- ✔ Reduces the number of mistakes you make as you type by intelligently and dynamically resizing the touch zones for certain keys.

Training your digits

Using the iPhone efficiently means that you need to master a few tricks: Tap, flick, swipe, and pinch:

- ✔ **Tap:** Tapping serves multiple purposes. Tap an icon to open an application from the Home screen, to start playing a song, or to choose the photo album you want to look through. Sometimes, you double-tap (twice in rapid succession) to zoom in or out of web pages, maps, and e-mails.

- ✔ **Swipe:** Swipe downward from the top of the screen and your iPhone displays the Notification

Center, where you can track all notifications you've received (including calls and voicemails, messages displayed by apps and even weather and stock figures). Many apps also allow you to browse photos and screens by swiping left and right across your screen.

- ✔ **Flick:** A flick of the finger on the screen lets you quickly scroll through lists of songs, e-mails, and picture thumbnails. Tap on the screen to stop scrolling, or merely wait for the scrolling list to stop.

- ✔ **Pinch/spread:** Place two fingers on the edges of a web page or picture to enlarge the images or make them smaller. Pinching and spreading are easy to master.

The Home screen discussed earlier in this part may not be the only screen of icons on your phone. When you start adding apps from the App Store, you may see two or more tiny dots between the Phone, Mail, Safari, and Music icons and the row of icons directly above them. These dots denote additional screens. The white dot indicates the screen you're currently viewing. To navigate between screens, either flick from right to left or left to right across the middle of the screen or tap directly on the dots.

The four icons in the last row — Phone, Mail, Safari, and Music — are in a special part of the screen known as the *dock*. When you switch from screen to screen as just described, these icons remain on the screen.

Press the Home button to jump back to the first screen of icons or the Home screen.

Finger typing

If you're patient and trusting, you'll get the hang of finger typing in a week or so. The virtual keyboard appears when you tap a text field to enter notes, compose text messages, type the names of new contacts, and so forth.

The keyboard does a pretty good job of coming up with the words you likely want to type next. As you press your finger against a letter or number on the screen, the individual key you press gets bigger and practically jumps off the screen, as shown in Figure 1-4. That way, you can see that you struck the correct letter or number. If you press and hold the .com key in Safari, it offers you the choice of .com, .net, .edu, .us, or .org.

Figure 1-4: The ABCs of virtual typing.

Mistakes are common at first. Say that you meant to type a sentence in the Notes app that reads, "I am typing a bunch of notes." But you actually entered "I am typing a bunch of *npyrs*." Fortunately, the iPhone knows that the *o* you meant to press is next to the *p* that showed up in your text, just as *t* and *y* and the *e* and the *r* are side by side. So the software determines that *notes* was indeed the word you had in mind and places it in red under the suspect word, as shown in Figure 1-5. To accept the suggested word, merely tap the Space key. And if you actually did intend to type *npyrs* instead, tap on the suggested word (*notes* in this example) to decline it.

When you're typing notes or sending e-mail and want to type a number, symbol, or punctuation mark, you have to tap the *123* key to bring up an alternative virtual keyboard. Tap the *ABC* key to return to the first keyboard. It's not hard to get used to, but some may find this extra step irritating.

You can rotate the iPhone so that its keyboard changes to a wider landscape mode in certain apps, including Mail, Messages, and Notes. The feature was already present in Safari. The keys are slightly larger in landscape mode, a potential boon to those who do a lot of typing or have largish fingers.

You can even dictate instead of wearing out your fingers! The Dictation key is to the left of the Space key — tap it any time you'd normally be typing and then begin speaking. Tap the Done icon to exit Dictation mode.

If you're using an iPhone 4s, 5, or 5s, you can also use your voice to dictate messages, notes, and reminders to *Siri* (the iPhone voice assistant).

Figure 1-5: The helpful keyboard.

Using Cut, Copy, Paste, and Replace

Apple brought three familiar friends from your computer — Cut, Copy, and Paste — to the iPhone. Apple also provides another remedy for correcting errors: the Replace pop-up option.

Say you're in the Notes app, jotting down ideas that you want to copy into an e-mail message. Double-tap a word to select it, and then drag the blue grab points or handles to select a block of text (see Figure 1-6). After you've selected the text, tap Copy. If you want to display a definition of the selected word, tap Define instead.

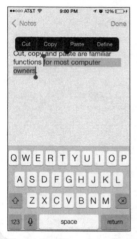

Figure 1-6: Drag the grab points to select text.

Now open the Mail program and start composing a message. When you decide where to insert the text you just copied, tap the cursor. Up pop commands to Select, Select All, and Paste, as shown in Figure 1-7. Tap Paste to paste the text into the message.

Anytime you notice an error in text you've typed or pasted, you can double-tap the word and the options change to Cut, Copy, and Paste (and, if you tap the right arrow next to Paste, you can choose Replace). Tap Replace and the iPhone serves up a few suggested replacement words. If the word you want to substitute is listed, tap it, and the iPhone automatically makes the switch.

Figure 1-7: Tap Paste to insert text.

Here's the cool part. If you make a mistake while you are cutting, pasting, replacing, or typing, shake the iPhone. It undoes the last edit.

Calling on the Control Center

iOS 7 marks the debut of the Control Center, where you can quickly and easily access the controls that most iPhone owners use most often. Swipe upward from the bottom of any screen to display the Control Center, shown in Figure 1-8. (You can even use the upward swipe gesture on the Lock screen, so you don't have to unlock your iPhone to use the Control Center.)

Figure 1-8: All your controls in one convenient spot.

The Control Center enables you to configure:

- ✔ **Wireless connections:** You can quickly turn your Wi-Fi and Bluetooth hardware on and off as needed, or toggle Do Not Disturb on and off.

- ✔ **Screen settings:** Choose a new brightness level or lock your iPhone's display orientation.

- ✔ **Music playback:** Display what track you're playing, pause it, fast-forward or reverse, or adjust the music volume.

- ✔ **AirDrop and AirPlay:** Exchange files with other iOS devices using AirDrop, or stream video to an Apple TV or other devices that support AirPlay.

- ✔ **Apps and functions:** Use your iPhone as a flashlight, display your calculator and countdown timer, or use your iPhone's camera.

Multitasking

Like your computer, your iPhone can handle more than one job at once. *Multitasking* simply lets you run numerous apps in the background simultaneously or switch easily from one app to another.

If you use an Internet voice-calling app such as Skype, you'll be able to receive notification of an incoming call even if you haven't launched the Skype app. The multitasking feature lets a navigation app employing GPS update your position while you're listening to an Internet radio app such as Pandora. From time to time, the navigation app will pipe in with turn-by-turn directions, lowering the volume of the music so you can hear the instructions.

Multitasking couldn't be easier. Double-press the Home button, and a row of screen thumbnails appears in the center of the screen, along with an icon representing the app that's running at the bottom of the screen. The thumbnails and icons represent the most recently used apps. Scroll to the right to see more apps. Tap the thumbnail you want to switch to: The app remembers where you left off.

To remove an app from the multitasking rotation, flick the screen thumbnail upward toward the top of your iPhone — and watch the offending app fly off the screen. Poof, it's gone.

Organizing with Folders

Finding the single app you want to use among apps spread out across 11 screens is a daunting task. Never fear, Apple includes a handy organization tool called Folders. This feature enables you to create folder icons, each holding up to a dozen apps.

To create a folder, press your finger against an icon until all the icons on the screen jiggle. Decide which apps you want to move to a folder, and drag the icon for the first app on top of the second app. The two apps now share living quarters inside a newly created folder. Apple names the folder according to the category of apps inside the folder, but you can easily change the folder name by tapping the X in the bar where the folder name appears and substituting a new name.

To launch an app that's inside a folder, tap that folder's icon and then tap the icon for the app that you want to open. In iOS 7, folders can contain multiple screens, so you'll have plenty of room for your apps. You'll see the familiar white dots that indicate which screen you're displaying within the folder.

You can drag apps into and out of any folder as long as there's room for them.

If you drag all the apps outside the folder, the folder automatically disappears.

Taking Your Best Shot

Camera phones may outsell dedicated digital cameras nowadays, but with relatively few exceptions, camera phones are rather mediocre picture-takers.

Using the camera

As with many apps on the iPhone, you find the Camera app icon on the Home screen beside the Photos app (unless you've moved things around). We tap both icons throughout this part. You might as well snap an image now:

1. **On the Home screen, tap the Camera app icon.**

2. **Keep your eyes fixed on the iPhone's display.**

   The display provides a window into what the camera lens sees.

3. **Aim the camera at whatever you want to shoot, using the iPhone's brilliant 4-inch display as your viewfinder.**

4. **When you're satisfied with what's in the frame, tap the round shutter icon at the bottom of the screen to snap the picture.**

To take a simple snapshot, make sure the dot at the bottom of the screen appears on the top of the Photo setting, instead of Video, Square, or Pano (short for Panoramic). Swipe the Mode control to the left or right as necessary to set the Camera mode.

iOS 7 also provides a Camera icon on the Lock screen, so there's no need to unlock your iPhone to take a quick snapshot. From the

Lock screen, drag the camera icon upward to reveal the Camera app.

Where have all my pictures gone?

So where exactly do your pictures hang out on the iPhone? The ones you snapped on the iPhone end up in a photo album appropriately dubbed the *Camera Roll*.

To view your photos, follow these steps:

1. **Tap the Photos icon on the Home screen and then tap the Camera Roll album or any other album that appears in the list of photo albums.**

2. **Browse through the thumbnail images in the album until you find the picture or video you want to display.**

   When a thumbnail represents a video rather than a still image, a tiny movie camera icon and the video length are displayed. If a particular thumbnail doesn't appear on this screen, flick your finger up or down to scroll through the pictures. Buttons at the bottom of the screen let you view Photos (collections of images and videos arranged by year, date, and location taken), Albums, and Shared Photo Streams (which use your iCloud account to send photos and videos to your Mac, PC and other iOS 5/6/7 devices).

3. **Tap the appropriate thumbnail.**

   The picture or video you selected fills the entire screen.

4. **Tap the screen again.**

   The picture controls appear.

5. To make the controls disappear, tap the screen again or just wait a few seconds and they go away on their own.

Deleting pictures

Fortunately, the iPhone makes it a cinch to bury bad photos:

1. From the Camera Roll, tap the objectionable photograph.

2. Tap to display the picture controls, if they're not already displayed.

3. Tap the trash can icon.

4. Tap Delete Photo (or Cancel, if you change your mind).

   The photo gets sucked into the trash can and mercifully disappears.

 To delete multiple photos and videos at once from an album or Photo Stream, tap the Select button and then tap each item thumbnail that you want to delete. Tap the trash can icon at the bottom of the Photos screen and then tap the Delete Photos button to confirm.

Mastering Video

The iPhone is not going to replace a high-definition television as the centerpiece of your home theater, but with its glorious widescreen display, watching movies and other videos on the iPhone can be a cinematic delight.

Playing video

When you feel like watching something, here's how to do it:

1. **On the Home screen, tap the Videos icon to bring up your list of videos.**

2. **Flick your finger to scroll through the list and then tap the video you want to play.**

   You may see a spinning circle for just a moment and then the video will begin.

3. **Turn the device on its side because the iPhone plays video only in landscape, or widescreen, mode.**

4. **Now that the video is playing, tap the screen to display the controls.**

5. **Tap the controls that follow as needed:**

   - To play or pause the video, tap the play/pause button.

   - Drag the volume slider to the right to raise the volume and to the left to lower it. Alternatively, use the physical volume buttons to control the audio levels.

   - Tap the restart/rewind button to restart the video; tap and hold the same button to rewind.

   - Tap and hold the fast-forward button to advance the video. Skip ahead by dragging the playhead along the Scrubber bar.

   - Tap the scale button to toggle between filling the entire screen with video or fitting the video to the screen.

6. **Tap the screen again to make the controls go away (or just wait for them to go away on their own).**

7. **Tap Done when you've finished watching.**

   You return to the iPhone's video menu screen.

To delete a video, tap the Edit button and then tap the small black Delete button (with the X) that materializes. To confirm your intention, tap the Delete button that appears.

Shooting video

Here's how to shoot video on your iPhone using iOS 7. Note that you can capture video in portrait or landscape mode:

1. **Tap the Camera icon on the Home screen.**

2. **Drag the Mode control to the right until the dot appears above the word Video.**

3. **Tap the red record button at the bottom center to begin shooting a scene.**

   The button blinks and you see a counter timing the length of your video.

4. **When you're finished, tap the red button again to stop recording.**

   Your video is automatically saved to the camera roll, alongside any other saved videos and still pictures.

Part II

Making Calls and Sending Messages

• •

In This Part

▶ Making a call

▶ Visualizing visual voicemail

▶ Sending and receiving text messages

▶ Using FaceTime to make a video call

• •

*T*he iPhone's most critical mission is the one from which its name is derived — it is first and foremost a cellphone. No matter how capable it is at all the other things, when push comes to shove, you had best be able to make and receive phone calls.

This part is devoted to the nifty ways you can handle wireless calls on an iPhone and keep in touch with text messages. We focus on the three types of iPhone message protocols: SMS, MMS, and iMessage.

Making a Call

Start by tapping the Phone icon on the Home screen. You can then make a call by tapping any of the icons that show up at the bottom of the screen: Favorites, Recents, Contacts, Keypad, or Voicemail, in that order. With the iPhone 4, you have one more way of calling — by using the aptly named Voice Control feature to dial a name or phone number by voice. Owners of an iPhone 4s, 5, and 5s can also use Siri, the voice assistant.

Keypad

From time to time, of course, you need to dial the number of a person or company that hasn't earned a spot in your Contacts. That's when you tap the Keypad icon to bring up the large keys of the virtual touchtone keypad. Just tap the appropriate keys and tap Call.

 To add this number to your address book, tap the Add to Contacts button that appears under the number.

Contacts

You get the mailing addresses, e-mail addresses, and phone numbers that reside on your PC or Mac into the iPhone by syncing or via iCloud (if you need help with these tasks, check out the full-sized book by John Wiley & Sons, Inc., *iPhone 5 For Dummies,* 7th Edition). Assuming that you've synced already, all those addresses and phone numbers are now hanging out in your Contacts. Tap the Phone icon on the Home screen and then tap Contacts, or tap the Contacts icon in the Utilities folder to see all your contact information.

Here's how to make these contacts work for you:

1. **Tap the Phone icon on the Home screen, and then tap Contacts.**

2. **Flick your finger so the list of contacts on the screen scrolls rapidly up or down, loosely reminiscent of a Las Vegas slot machine.**

Alternatively, you can move your finger along the alphabet on the right edge of the Contacts list or tap one of the tiny letters to jump to names that begin with that letter. You also can find a list of potential matches by starting to type the name of a contact in the search field near the top of the list.

3. **When you're at or near the appropriate contact name, stop the scrolling by tapping the screen.**

4. **Tap the name of the person you want to call.**

As shown in Figure 2-1, you can see a bunch of fields with the individual's phone numbers, FaceTime information, physical and e-mail addresses, and possibly even a mug shot.

Figure 2-1: I figured this contact would already be there.

5. **Tap the phone icon next to the desired number, and the iPhone initiates the call.**

Your own iPhone phone number, lest you forget it, appears at the top of the Contacts list, provided you arrived in Contacts by way of the Phone application.

Voice dialing

With the iPhone 4, you can make a hands-free call simply by opening your mouth. To summon Voice Control, press and hold the Home button, or press and hold the center button on the wired headset supplied with the iPhone.

Wait for the tone and speak clearly, especially if you're in a noisy environment. You can dial by number, as in "Dial 202-555-1212;" you can dial by name, as in "Call Bob LeVitus;" or you can be a tad more specific as in "Dial Bob LeVitus mobile." Before actually dialing the number, an automated female voice repeats what she thinks you said.

If the person you're calling has multiple phone numbers and you fail to specify which one, the female voice will prompt you, "Ed Baig, home, mobile, or work?" Tell her which one it is, or say "Cancel" if you decide not to call.

Conversing with Siri

The iPhone 4s, 5, and 5s can use *Siri*, the iPhone voice assistant, which provides you with enhanced control over all sorts of iPhone tasks. (Think "Voice Control" after your iPhone has undergone a *serious* college education.)

Siri requires a Wi-Fi or 3G/4G/LTE connection to the Internet.

You activate Siri in the same way as Voice Control on older iPhones. Press and hold the Home button — after you hear the tone, you can issue a command or ask Siri, "What can you do?" (Take our word for it, the response you'll get is a real eye-opener!) Again, the quieter the environment, the better.

Unlike Voice Control, Siri's capabilities extend far beyond just voice dialing and playing music. You can control virtually all of the important apps on your iPhone — and you can launch many apps directly by simply saying "Launch" followed by the app name (such as "Launch Music"). For example, try out these commands:

- **Safari:** "Search the Web for…"
- **Maps:** "How do I get to…"
- **FaceTime:** "FaceTime Bob"
- **Messages:** "Tell my Dad…"
- **Calendar:** "Make an appointment…"

Siri is intelligent enough to recognize different verbs for the same action, like "Tell Bob to sell 20 shares" or "Send a message to Bob saying sell 20 shares." (Are you starting to feel like George Jetson right about now?)

Like Voice Control, Siri audibly confirms your command — but she also displays your command on the screen and the response she wants to make. Siri displays a thumbnail for the corresponding app, along with related information (for example, the text of an e-mail message you've asked Siri to read). You can tap this information display to launch the app directly.

While Siri is active, you can issue another command or clarify your request by tapping the microphone icon at the bottom of the screen. (Like any good assistant, Siri allows you to add, cancel, or change information before acting on your command.)

Visual voicemail

How often have you had to listen to several voicemail messages before getting to the message you really want to hear? As shown in Figure 2-2, the iPhone's clever visual voicemail presents a list of your voicemail messages in the order in which calls were received. But you need not listen to those messages in order.

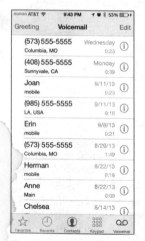

Figure 2-2: Visual voicemail in action.

How do you even know you have voicemail? There are a few ways:

- ✔ A red circle showing the number of pending messages appears above the Phone icon on the Home screen or above the Voicemail icon from within the Phone application.

- ✔ You may also see a notification on the iPhone display that says something like, "New voicemail from Ed."

Whatever draws you in, tap that Voicemail icon to display the list of voicemails. You see the caller's phone number, assuming this information is known through CallerID, and in some cases, his or her name. Or, you see the word *Unknown*.

A blue dot next to a name or number signifies that you haven't heard the message yet.

To play back a voicemail, tap the name or number in question. Tap the Pause icon to pause the message; tap again to resume. Tap the Speaker button if you want to hear the message through the iPhone's speakerphone. To replay the message, tap the Play button.

 Tap the blue Info icon (the lowercase "i" in a circle) next to a caller's name or number to bring up any contact info on the person or to add the caller to your Contacts.

 The tiny playhead along the Scrubber bar (refer to Figure 2-2) shows you the length of the message and how much of the message you've heard. If you hate when callers ramble on, drag the playhead to rapidly advance through a message. If you miss something, you can replay that segment.

Tap the Call Back button to immediately return the call. If the caller's number is unknown, the Call Back button appears dimmed. Delete a voicemail by pressing Delete. If you have no phone service, you see a message that says *Visual Voicemail is currently unavailable.*

You can listen to your iPhone voicemail from another phone. Just dial your iPhone number and, while the greeting plays, enter your voicemail password. You can set up such a password from the Home screen by tapping Settings, and then tapping Phone, Change Voicemail Password. You're asked to enter your current voicemail password if you have one. If one doesn't exist yet, tap Done. If it does exist, enter it and then tap Done. You're then asked to type the new password and tap Done, twice.

Recording a greeting

You have two choices when it comes to the voicemail greeting your callers hear. You can accept a generic greeting with your phone number by default. Or, you can create a custom greeting in your own voice as follows:

1. **In the Voicemail application, tap the Greeting button.**

2. **Tap Custom.**

3. **Tap Record; then dictate a clever, deserving-of-being-on-the-iPhone greeting.**

4. **When you have finished recording, tap Stop.**

5. **Review the greeting by pressing Play.**

6. **If the greeting is worthy, tap Save. If not, tap Cancel and start over at Step 1.**

Receiving a Call

It's wonderful to have numerous options for making a call. But what are your choices when somebody calls you? The answer depends on whether you are willing to take the call or not. Luckily, the iPhone includes caller ID display for those numbers in your Contacts list.

Accepting the call

To accept a call, you have several options:

- ✔ Tap Answer and greet the caller.
- ✔ If the phone is locked, drag the Answer slider to the right.
- ✔ Tap the Respond with Text button to send a text message or iMessage to the caller.
- ✔ Tap the Remind Me Later button to display a reminder to call the person back.
- ✔ If you are using the stereo earbuds that come with the iPhone, tap the microphone button.

WARNING!

If you are listening to music in your iPhone's Music app when a call comes in, the song stops playing and you have to decide whether to take the call. If you do take the call, the music resumes where it left off when the conversation ends.

Rejecting the call

Here are three ways to reject a call on the spot and send the call to voicemail:

- ✔ Tap Decline.

- ✔ Press the sleep/wake button twice in rapid succession. (The button is on the top of the device.)

- ✔ Using the supplied headset, press and hold the microphone button for a couple of seconds and then let go. Two beeps let you know that the call was rejected.

Sometimes you're perfectly willing to take a call but you need to silence the ringer or turn off the vibration. Just press the sleep/wake button a single time, or press one of the volume buttons. Then answer the call.

iOS 7 also includes *Do Not Disturb*, which you can configure within Settings. When you turn on Do Not Disturb within the top Settings screen (or from the Control Center), all alerts and ringtones are turned off. (You can also specify just a handful of contacts that can reach you no matter what.)

Messaging

The Messages application lets you exchange short text messages with any cellphone that supports the SMS protocol. If you own any iPhone except the original version and are using at least iOS 3.0, you can also send and receive MMS messages, which let you exchange pictures, contacts, videos, ringtones, other audio recordings, and locations with any cellphone that supports the MMS protocol. Finally, if you're using any iPhone that's running iOS 5 or later, you can send iMessages with text, video, or audio — free of charge — to any other device running iOS 5 or later. (The list includes another iPhone, an iPad, or an iPod touch, as well as a Mac running OS X Lion or later.)

The intelligent virtual keyboard makes it easy to compose short text messages, and the big, bright high-resolution screen makes it a pleasure to read them. (On an iPhone 4s, 5, 5s/5c, you can even command Siri to create a text message for you using only your voice!)

Here are some messaging basics for SMS/MMS:

- ✔ **Both sender and receiver need SMS- or MMS-enabled mobile phones.** Your iPhone qualifies, as does almost any mobile phone made in the past few years. Keep in mind that if you send messages to folks with phones that don't support SMS or MMS, or to those who choose not to pay extra for messaging services, they will never get your message or even know you sent a message.

- ✔ **Some phones (not the iPhone, of course) limit SMS messages to 160 characters.** If you try to send a longer message to one of these phones, your message may be cut off or split into multiple shorter messages. So keep SMS messages brief.

- ✔ **Most iPhone plans no longer include SMS or MMS messages.** You'll be billed for individual SMS or MMS text messages unless you subscribe to the unlimited texting plan. (Note that MMS is available from AT&T at no additional cost to customers with an SMS text-messaging bundle.)

Each individual message in a conversation counts against this total, even if it's only a one-word reply such as "OK" or "CUL8R" (which is text-speak for "see you later").

✔ **You can send or receive messages only over your wireless carrier's network.** In other words, SMS and MMS messages can't be sent or received over a Wi-Fi connection — however, iMessage works fine over both Wi-Fi and cellular connections.

Okay, now that you know the messaging basics, here's how to send a message.

Sending an SMS message

Tap the Messages icon on the Home screen to launch the Messages application; then tap the little pencil-and-paper icon in the top-right corner of the screen to start a new text message.

At this point, the To field is active and awaiting your input. You can do three things at this point:

✔ If the recipient isn't in your Contacts list, type his or her cellphone number.

✔ If the recipient *is* in your Contacts list, type the first few letters of the name. A list of matching contacts appears. Scroll through it if necessary and tap the name of the contact.

✔ Tap the blue + icon on the right side of the To field to select a name from your Contacts list.

To enter your text, tap in the text entry box (next to the camera icon). When you've finished addressing and composing, tap the Send button to send your message on its merry way.

Receiving an SMS message

If you want an alert to sound when you receive a message, tap the Settings icon on your Home screen, tap Sounds, tap the Text Tone item, and then tap one of the available sounds. You can audition the sounds by tapping them.

You won't hear a sound when a message arrives if the Ring/Silent switch is set to Silent, or if you've turned on the Do Not Disturb feature. (Your iPhone still displays a notification, however.)

If you don't want to hear an alert when a message arrives, tap the first item in the list: None.

If you receive a message when your phone is asleep, all or part of the text message and the name of the sender appear on the Unlock screen when you wake your phone.

If your phone is awake and unlocked when a message arrives, all or part of the message and the name of the sender appear at the top of the screen (as well as in the Notification Center, which you can display by swiping downward from the top of the screen). At the same time, the Messages icon on the Home screen displays the number of unread messages.

You can, however, set your iPhone to display an alert (which enables you to reply immediately). Tap Settings, tap Notification Center, and then tap the Messages entry and choose the Alerts setting. Now that you can read or reply to a text message, tap Reply when the message appears (see Figure 2-3).

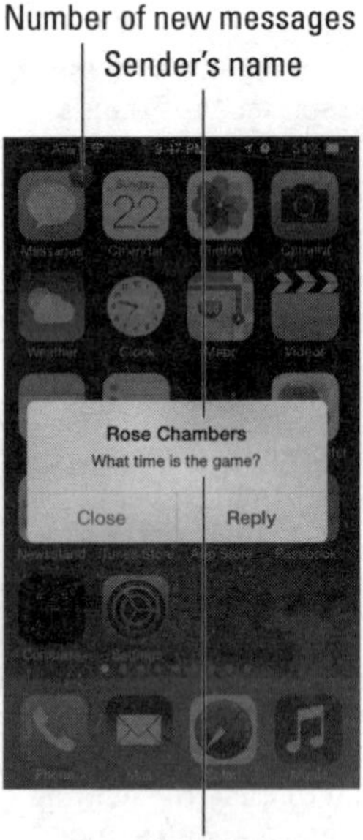

Number of new messages
Sender's name

Message

Figure 2-3: What you see if your iPhone is set to alert notification when a message arrives.

If you're not using alerts, tap the Messages icon to read or reply to a message. If a message other than the one you're interested in appears onscreen when you launch Messages, tap Messages in the top-left corner of the screen, and then tap the recipient's name; that person's messages appear on the screen.

To reply to the message on the screen, tap the text-entry field to the left of the Send button, and the keyboard appears. Type your reply and then tap Send.

 Tap the Dictation key — the key to the left of Space, which bears a microphone symbol — and you can dictate text directly into the text-entry field! Tap the Done button to watch the magic happen.

Your conversation is saved as a series of text bubbles. Your messages appear on the right side of the screen in green bubbles; the other person's messages appear on the left in gray bubbles, as shown in Figure 2-4.

You can delete a conversation in two ways:

✔ **If you're viewing the conversation:** Tap and hold your finger on any message in the conversation, and you'll see a number of circles appear to the left of each message. Now you can delete the entire conversation by tapping the Delete All button in the top-left corner of the screen.

✔ **If you're viewing the list of text messages:** Tap the Edit button at the top left of the Messages list, tap the red dash (—) icon that appears to the left of the person's name, and then tap the Delete button that appears to the right of the name.

What they said

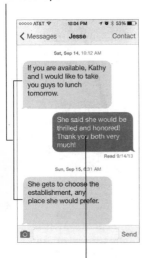

What you said

Figure 2-4: An SMS conversation.

MMS: Like SMS with media

To send a picture or video in a message, follow the instructions for sending a text message and then tap the camera icon to the left of the text-entry field at the bottom of the screen. You have the option of using an existing picture or video or taking a new one. You can also add text to photos or videos. When you're finished, tap the Send button.

If you receive a picture or video in a message, it appears in a bubble just like text. Tap it to see it full-screen.

Tap the icon in the lower-left corner (the one that looks like an arrow trying to escape from a rectangle) for additional options. If you don't see the icon, tap the picture or video once and the icon magically appears.

iMessage: iOS 5/6/7 messaging

Although the party is limited to owners of iOS 5, 6, and 7 devices, iMessage provides everything that MMS includes — video, locations, contacts, and photos — and iMessages can be sent over a Wi-Fi connection as well as a cellular connection. Plus, they're as free as the air around you!

iMessage operates just like MMS. To verify that you're using iMessage, check the information line at the top of a conversation — it should read *iMessage*. You also see the word *iMessage* in the text entry box.

Seeing Is Believing with FaceTime

Using FaceTime video calling is as easy as making a regular call on the iPhone. Plus, FaceTime comes with at least two major benefits *besides* the video factor:

- ✔ FaceTime calls don't count against your regular plan minutes.

- ✔ The audio quality on FaceTime calls is superior to a regular cellphone connection.

But FaceTime also has a couple of major caveats:

- ✔ Both you and the party you're talking to must have an iPhone 4 or later, a Mac (running OS X Snow Leopard or later), or an iOS device compatible with FaceTime (like an iPad 2/3 or iPod touch). FaceTime doesn't work with older models of the iPhone.

- ✔ Both you and the caller at the other end must be accessing either Wi-Fi or a 3G/4G/LTE cellular connection. The quality of the experience depends on a solid connection.

If you meet the requirements, here's how to make FaceTime happen:

1. **The first time you make a FaceTime call, dial the person's regular iPhone number using any of the methods described earlier.**

2. **When a regular call is established and you've broached the subject of going video, tap the FaceTime button.**

   A few seconds later, the other person gets the option to Decline or Answer by tapping the red button or the green button, respectively. If you choose Answer, you need to wait a few seconds before you can see the other person. In the same fashion as receiving a voice call, iOS 7 also allows you to decline the call with a reminder to return the call, or decline the call and reply instead with a text message.

If you want to mute a FaceTime call, tap the microphone icon with the slash running through it. The caller is still connected, but cannot hear you. To hide the Mute, Switch Camera, and End buttons, just tap any part of the image.

Part III

Surfing and Using E-Mail

- -

In This Part

▶ Surfing the 'Net

▶ Opening and displaying web pages

▶ Setting up your e-mail accounts

▶ Sending e-mail messages

- -

*W*ith the iPhone, Apple has managed, for the most part, to replicate the real-deal Internet. Web pages on the iPhone look like web pages on a Windows PC or Mac, right down to swanky graphics and pictures and some video. In this part, you find out how to navigate cyberspace on your iPhone.

Surfin' Safari

A special version of the Safari web browser on the iPhone is a big reason the web on the iPhone is much like the web you've come to expect on your computer.

Exploring the browser

It's worth starting this cyber-expedition with a quick tour of the Safari browser. Take a gander at Figure 3-1.

Figure 3-1: The iPhone's Safari browser.

Blasting into cyberspace

When you tap the address field at the top of the Safari browser, the virtual keyboard appears. You may notice one thing about the keyboard right off the bat: the period (.) is on the virtual keyboard because you frequently use periods when you enter web addresses.

The moment you tap a single letter, you see web addresses that match those letters. For example, if you tap the letter *s,* you may see web listings for Si.com, Scholastic.com, and CNET Shopper, among others. Scroll to see more suggestions, and the virtual keyboard slides off the screen.

Go ahead and open your first web page now:

1. **Tap the Safari icon at the bottom of the Home screen.**

2. **Tap the address field.**

   If you can't see the address field, tap the site name at the top of the screen or flick down to scroll to the top of the screen.

3. **Begin typing the web address on the virtual keyboard that slides up from the bottom of the screen.**

4. **Do one of the following:**

   a. *To accept one of the bookmarked (or other) sites that show up on the list, merely tap the name.*

      Safari automatically puts the URL in the address field and takes you where you want to go.

   b. *Keep tapping the proper keyboard characters until you enter the complete web address for the site you want; then tap Go in the lower-right corner of the keyboard.*

      It's not necessary to type *www* at the beginning of a URL. So, if you want to visit www.theonion. com, typing **theonion.com** or even **onion.com** is sufficient.

Even though Safari on the iPhone can render web pages the way they're meant to be displayed on a computer, every so often you run into a site that will serve up a mobile version of the website. Graphics may be stripped down on these sites. (For example, CNN.com detects the mobile version of Safari when you visit and presents a simplified site.)

Seeing Pages More Clearly

Here's how radically simple it is to zoom in on pages. Try these neat tricks:

- ✔ **Double-tap the screen so that the portion of the text you want to read fills the entire screen.** Check out Figure 3-2. It shows two views of the same *New York Times* web page. In the first view, you see what the page looks like when you first open it. In the second one, you see how the picture takes over much more of the screen after you double-tap it. To return to the first view, double-tap the screen again.

- ✔ **Pinch the page.** Sliding your thumb and index finger together and then spreading them apart also zooms in and out of a page.

Figure 3-2: A double-tap zooms in and out.

- ✔ **Press down on a page and drag it in all directions, or flick through a page from top to bottom.**

- ✔ **Rotate the iPhone to its side.** Watch what happens to the National Geographic website shown in Figure 3-3. It reorients from portrait to a widescreen view.

Figure 3-3: Going wide.

Setting Up E-Mail

To use Mail, the iPhone's e-mail app, you need an e-mail address. If you have broadband Internet access (that is, a cable modem or DSL), you probably received one or more e-mail addresses when you signed up.

(Apple also gives you a free iCloud email address when you create an Apple ID.) If you are one of the handful of readers who doesn't already have an e-mail account, you can get one for free from Yahoo! (http://mail.yahoo.com), Google (http://mail.google.com), AOL (www.aol.com), Apple's iCloud (www.apple.com/icloud), Microsoft (Outlook.com), or one of many other service providers.

If you have no e-mail accounts on your iPhone, the first time you launch Mail, you're walked through the following procedure. If you have one or more e-mail accounts on your iPhone already and want to add a new account manually, start by tapping Settings on the Home screen, and then tap Mail, Contacts, Calendars, and Add Account.

Yahoo!, Google, Microsoft, AOL, or iCloud

If your account is with Apple's own iCloud service, Microsoft Exchange, Microsoft Outlook.com, Google's Gmail, Yahoo!, or AOL, tap the appropriate button on the Add Account screen. If your account is with a provider other than the ones listed, tap the Other button and skip to the next section. Enter your name, e-mail address, and password, as shown in Figure 3-4 (these are the fields required for a Google Gmail account). The description field is usually filled in automatically with the content you have in the address field, but you can replace that text with your own description (such as Work or Personal).

Tap the Next button in the upper-right corner of the screen. Your e-mail provider verifies your credentials. If you pass muster, that's all there is to setting up your account.

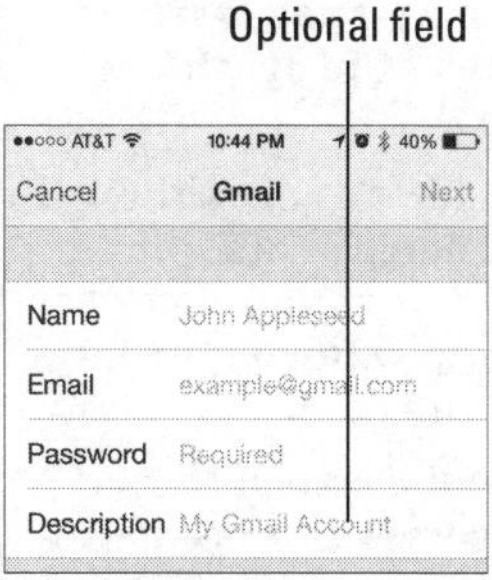

Optional field

Figure 3-4: Just fill 'em in and tap Next.

Another provider

If your e-mail account is with a provider other than
iCloud, Microsoft, Gmail, Yahoo!, or AOL, you have a
bit more work ahead of you. If your account can't be
verified within Settings, you're going to need a bunch
of information about your e-mail account that you may
not know or have handy.

Scan the following instructions, note the items you
don't know, and go find the answers before you continue. To find the answers, look at the documentation
you received when you signed up for your e-mail
account or visit the account provider's website and
search there.

Here's how you set up an account:

1. **On the Add Account screen, tap the Other
   button.**

2. **Under Mail, tap Add Mail Account. Fill in the
   name, address, password, and description in the**

appropriate fields, the same as if you were setting up an account with one of the providers
mentioned earlier. Tap Next.

With any luck, that's all you have to do, although
you may have to endure a spinning cursor for a
while as the iPhone attempts to retrieve information and validate your account with your provider. Otherwise, continue with Step 3.

3. **Tap the button at the top of the screen that
   denotes the type of e-mail server this account
   uses: IMAP or POP.**

4. **Fill in the Internet host name for your incoming
   mail server, which should look something like
   mail.*providername*.com.**

5. **Fill in your username and password.**

6. **Enter the Internet host name for your outgoing
   mail server, which should look something like
   smtp.*providername*.com.**

   You may have to scroll down to the bottom of the
   screen to see the outgoing mail server fields.

7. **Enter your username and password in the appropriate fields.**

8. **Tap the Next button in the upper-right corner to
   create the account.**

Sending E-Mail

To compose a new e-mail message, tap Mail on the
Home screen to open the Mailboxes screen or whichever screen was up when you last left the app. Then
follow these steps:

1. **Tap the New Message button in the lower-right corner of the screen.**

   The button appears on all the Mail screens, so don't worry if you're not at the main Mailboxes screen. A screen like the one shown in Figure 3-5 appears.

Figure 3-5: The New Message screen.

2. **Type the names or e-mail addresses of the recipients in the To field or tap the + button to the right of the To field to select a contact or contacts from your iPhone's address book.**

   If you start typing an e-mail address, e-mail addresses that match what you typed appear in a list below the To or Cc field. If the correct one is in the list, tap it to use it.

3. **Type a subject in the Subject field.**

4. **Type your message in the message area.**

5. **Tap the Send button in the upper-right corner of the screen.**

Your message wings its way to its recipients almost immediately. If you aren't in range of a Wi-Fi network, the AT&T EDGE, or 3G/4G/LTE data network when you tap Send, the message is sent the next time you're in range of one of these networks.

Reading messages

Tap the Mail icon now to summon the Mailboxes screen. At the top of the Inboxes section is the All Inboxes inbox, which, as its name suggests, is a repository for all the messages across all your accounts. To read your mail, tap an inbox: either All Inboxes to examine all your messages in one unified view, or an individual account to check out messages from just that account.

Now tap a message to read it. When a message is on the screen, buttons for managing incoming messages appear below it.

Replying to or forwarding a message

When you receive a message and want to reply to it, open the message and then tap the Reply/Reply All/ Forward icon (which looks like an arrow curving to the left). Then tap the Reply, Reply All, or Forward button.

The Reply button creates a new e-mail message addressed to the sender of the original message. The

Reply All button (which appears with multiple recipients only) creates an outgoing e-mail message addressed to the sender and all other recipients of the original message.

Tapping the Forward button creates an unaddressed e-mail message that contains the text of the original message. Add the e-mail address(es) of the person or people you want to forward the message to and then tap Send.

 Don't forget that snappy Dictation key on your iPhone's virtual keyboard! If you're running iOS 5 (or later), tap the key with the micro-phone symbol and begin speaking. When you're through dictating the message, tap the Done button.

To send your reply or forwarded message, tap the Send button as usual.

Identifying new messages

You can tell when you have unread mail by looking at the Mail icon at the bottom of your Home screen. The cumulative number of unread messages across all your e-mail inboxes appears in a little red circle in the upper-right area of the icon. New message notifications also appear on the Notification Center; swipe down from the top of the screen to display it.

Managing messages

When a message is on your screen, you can do many tasks in addition to reading it. The following buttons perform these various stunts:

✔ View the next message by tapping the next message arrow at the upper-right corner of the screen. It's the downward-pointing arrow.

✔ View the preceding message by tapping the previous message arrow (the one pointing upward).

✔ Flag this message by tapping the Flag button, which looks like. . . well. . . a flag. You can choose to flag the message, mark it as unread, or move it to your Junk box for the current account. (When you flag a message, it appears in the Inbox list with a flag icon to the left of the entry. You can use flags to mark important messages that need immediate follow-up.)

✔ File this message in another folder by tapping the file message icon. When the list of folders appears, tap the folder where you want to file the message.

✔ Delete this message by tapping the delete message icon (represented by the now-familiar trash can). You have to dig in the trash to retrieve the message if you tap the delete message icon by mistake.

✔ Reply, reply to all, or forward this message by tapping the Reply/Reply All/Forward icon.

✔ Create a new e-mail message by tapping the new message icon.